DANDELION WISHES

THERESE M. GUY

Omaha, Nebraska

©2021 Therese M. Guy
All Rights Reserved.

No part of this publication may be reproduced, stored in a retrieval system, or transmitted in any form or by any means—electronic, mechanical, photocopy, recording, or any other, except for brief quotations in printed reviews, without the prior permission from the publisher.

For inquiries, contact: Turtlewoman@conciergemarketing.com

Paperback 978-1-7359949-1-8
Kindle 978-1-7359949-1-8
EPUB 978-1-7359949-1-8

Library of Congress Cataloging Number: 2020920636

Illustrated by the author
Publishing and Production by Concierge Publishing Services

Printed in the United States of America
10 9 8 7 6 5 4 3 2 1

To all my fellow warriors.
You are truly people of substance.

CONTENTS

- DANDELION WISHES 3
- SCENIC ROUTE 4
- SPRING-CLEANING 5
- JUNK 6
- A LITTLE WINE WITH THAT CHEESE 8
- THE ROSE 9
- WALK-ABOUT 10
- TALK IT OUT 11
- EXTORTION 12
- SPRING'S SAVING GRACE 13
- I HATE GEORGE 14
- IMAGINE A WORLD 16
- TAX MAN 18
- UNCLE SAM, I AM 20
- PUSH SLIDE TAP 22
- FACEBOOK 23
- FLESHY SHELL 24
- SELF CHATTER 25
- IT FOLLOWED ME HOME 26
- HOUSE CATS 28
- EFFORT 29
- WAR OF THE STREETS 30
- OLD WAYS 32
- LESS THAN 33
- RESPECT: TO HOLD IN HIGH REGARD .. 34
- POTENTIAL 36
- PERSEVERE 37
- DON'T TALK CRAP 38
- I MOVE LIKE A TURTLE 40
- THE TROUBLE WITH CAN'T 41
- CAROUSEL 42
- I GET UP 44
- WHEN 46
- CONTROL 47
- POETRY 48
- WRITER'S BLOCK 49
- TO WRITE OR NOT TO WRITE? 50
- THE TREE 52
- THE TRUTH OF THE MATTER 54
- THE DEATH OF DREAMS 56
- SLEEPLESS 58
- SLEEP 59
- FAMILY PHOTOS 60
- IRELAND 61
- HEAVY LOAD 62
- IN THE COURTYARD 64
- GRATITUDE 65
- MY MOTHER'S DISHES 66
- MY MOTHER'S CLOSET 67
- ONCE I WAS BEAUTIFUL. 68
- THE ULTIMATE BETRAYAL 69
- QUARANTINE 70
- FLU 72
- WORDS 74
- NEGATIVE POSTS 75
- TRAVELER 76
- MIDWEST 77
- APRIL'S FOOLS 78
- CROSSWORDS 79
- OUT HOUSE 80
- NEW YEAR 82
- EMPTY WELL 83
- THE FENCE WALKER 84
- I RUN WITH A GANG 86
- I USED TO BE STRONG 87
- WINTER'S TOUCH 88
- ORDINARY LIFE 89
- TEA PARTY 90
- CHALK 92
- CRAYON MARKS 93
- AFTER THE PARADES 95
- EVERY GENERATION 96
- ALL OF THOSE 98
- IT'S A GOOD LIFE 99
- I MARRIED A PIRATE 100
- FRIENDS ARE LIKE SHOES 102
- BUCKET LIST 103
- CHOOSE 104
- BOB AND WEAVE 106
- HEADING TO THE Y 107
- FIRE SPINNING 108
- TEACHER 109

DANDELION WISHES

The girl picked up the seeded dandelion
And blew with all her might
Her wishes and dreams took flight

Over the chain-linked fences they flew
Across trash-filled streets
On the breeze, they leaped and pranced
With the grace of athletes danced

And while she concentrated, eye's shut tight
Her hearts desire upon the wind
Life's hard knock's could not rescind
Cause that day---there was magic in the air

SCENIC ROUTE

I have navigational limitations
Directional challenges
The paths morph into mutations

I have a tendency to take the scenic route

I have a planned destination
An end goal
A definite location

Somehow I end up on the scenic route

I'm not afraid to ask directions
I can read the signs, follow a map
But focus blurs and becomes an aberration

And I find myself on the scenic route

I understand others frustrations
At the roadblocks, pit stops
Delaying their debarkation
But I say, "Sit back, relax, enjoy the scenic route."

Detours are a part of any expedition
Turnabouts exist on most routes
They happen on all epic excursions

Just shrug your shoulders and do what I do,
Take the Scenic Route

SPRING-CLEANING

Time to Spring clean
I wear procrastination
Like a warm coat tight across
My shoulders.
Cocooning lethargy
Time to open the windows
And let the crisp, clean air
Reinvigorate my soul
Sweep out apathy
Blow on the coals
And ignite the fire
Renewing my vigor
Throw out lassitude
With the trash

JUNK

I have a plethora of junk
Both in the physical realm
And in the mental domain

I'm starting a campaign
To clean house
Downsize, sanitize, simplify

To the garbage say goodbye
Throw out the trash
If it's not necessary, it doesn't stay

Uh, well…I might need that one-day
Not that, too many memories
That'sss…an heirloom

I've had it since the womb
That grudge is under lock and key
Those tears a part of my hoard

I don't think I can sever the chord
It's all gotta go, I know
So hard to part
Tomorrow I'll get an early start

A LITTLE WINE WITH THAT CHEESE

I must confide

I can no longer abide

The Whine

Leads to cheese

The cheese to whatever I please

Which is all fattening

Even in misery

There is comfort in familiarity

I carry obesity

In the pocket of my genes

It takes a heavy toll

Its tenacity sticks to my soul

Like gum on the bottom of my shoe

I must stop the tantrum

Food no longer my anthem

I must surrender the anger

It attacks like a grizzly

The results I can no longer bare

I must be the master of fate

Adjust my gait

And toe the line

THE ROSE

The rose that grew through concrete

Does not know defeat

It knows not only strife

But the true value of life

It does not recognize the concept of retreat

The rose that grew through concrete

Does not listen to the under Lord's deceit

It knows that it is Love

Nurtured not of Earth, but from above

And therefore death it cheats

The rose that grew through concrete

Quite a monumental feat

From pain it has no immunity

It simply had opportunity

Doubter's shouts it beat

A rose that grows through concrete

Does not need to be elite

It only needs the Son's light

To win the fight

And rise up off the street

WALK-ABOUT

Some---
When life's hardships require respite
Travel
They go on a walkabout
'Til mind and body unite
The racing mind
Slows to keep beat
With journeying feet

I---I
When from cluttered thoughts need reprieve
Talk
I go on a talk about
I find a friendly ear
Maybe not even human
Babble acting as balm
Torrents of thoughts turn to calm

TALK IT OUT

Scream and shout
Just communicate
Release the floodgate

But how does one accomplish the task
Of removing the glued-on mask
No idea what-so-ever
The Id so strong and clever

It's created its own language
To give it an advantage
The laugh strong and hearty
Really a private pity party

Talk it out
In the debris, cast about
Don't stop the search
Continue the research

Zero in like a sniper
Break the code, and decipher
End the drought
And just talk it out

EXTORTION

Ding Ding

Ding Ding

The Ice Cream truck

Was coming

I raced into my room

Dang, my piggy bank

Was empty

Ding Ding

It was getting closer

My older brother was watching me

Well, suppose to be

Ding Ding

Oh crap, only four houses away

"Bill, give me a dime!"

"What, brat, no way!"

Ding Ding

I was getting desperate

"If you don't, I'll tell Dad."

"Tell Dad what?"

"That you stole a cigarette from his pack."

Ding Ding

The dime flew across the room

I caught it midair

And scrambled out the door

To catch the Ice Cream man

And that was my first

Successful extortion

SPRING'S SAVING GRACE

April slowly weans
of winters bitter chill
Teasing us with bits of green
When can we expect the daffodil
Frost's bite we've had our fill
The Robin's song
Gives hope to weary hearts
The cold weather is not long
As winter departs
Gentle rain starts
Jackets replace coats
A warm wind blows
The warmth denotes
Suns radiance glows
The gardener sows
A small bud forms
The dormant arise
A world transforms
Our angst tranquilize
With Earth's soft sighs
As Spring arrives
Our dreams renew
As nature survives
We amend our dismal view
Ah, Spring, life anew

I HATE GEORGE

I hate George

I hate his machinations

Although I have not capitulated

Nor bowed down in homage to him

But, I have paid

Yes, I have paid

I hate George

I hate my need of him

Although I stand autonomous

Nor joined the cult worshipers

But I hunger

Yes, I crave nourishment

I hate George

I hate his power

Although lives have been sacrificed

For him

Won for him

Souls have been traded

For him

I have slaved

For him

I hate George

I hate my weakness

But today I'm cold

Yes, sought after warmth propels me
To go to work
To earn George
Another Damn Dollar

IMAGINE A WORLD

Imagine a World where words of anger were forbidden
Negative thoughts did not come unbidden
Then again
 I do enjoy a good argument
Allows the steam to vent
Imagine a world where thoughts were clear
And comebacks you did not fear
Then again
I like a sharp wit
So that I would not omit
Imagine a world were problems were not as big as mountains
Then again
Therein lies the paradigm
Because I like a good climb
Imagine a world without strife
No struggles in our life
Then again
Without adversity
How do I gauge my fortitude
Imagine a world without tears
All sorrow disappears
Then again
Would I know great joy

Imagine a world where all your dreams came true
You got your due
Then again
Where would be purpose
Imagine a world imperfect
Then again
Much to my dismay
It's where I prefer to stay

TAX MAN

Hey tax man
I am not a fan

You're taxing my nerves
Depleting my reserves

I am aware
Of the street repair

But elsewhere
Is not done with care

In fact an epic fail
A very sad tale

The burden is heavy
With each levy

On your average Joe
A tough row to hoe

Income, sales, home and gas
Sanity it does surpass

Next, it will be the air we breathe
It just makes me seethe

Please we need a reprieve
Don't be naive

Many agree
Into the harbor with the tea

The rich with their loopholes
Is taking a toll

If representation is AWOL
Our system will fall

It needs an overhaul
Do not dally, do not stall

Give us a break
A lot is at stake

I am not alone
You must atone

Self-preservation
In over taxation

Leads to revolution
There is a solution

Make haste
No time to waste

Change now

Uncle Sam, I Am

Uncle Sam, I Am
I do not like the candidates
The utter insanity of the debates
What a lot of flim-flam
Uncle Sam, I Am
I do not like their pretense
What a lot of nonsense
What a sham
Uncle Sam, I Am
I do not like them in Alaska
I do not like them in Nebraska
Not even in Birmingham
Uncle Sam, I Am
Their words how do I rate
When the very next ones do negate
I'm sorry I'm a doubting Thomas
I don't believe their promise
I do not like them in Tennessee
I do not like them in Waikiki
Wish they would get with the program
Uncle Sam, I Am
On ideas they seem lax
I don't think I can bear one more tax
With each other mud does sling
But no solutions does it bring
I think they need a diagram
Uncle Sam, I Am
I do not like them in the dark of night
I do not like them by dawn's early light

I need someone to trust in the fight
Who do I go with, the lion or the lamb
Uncle Sam, I Am
I do not like the State of Union
Right now the state of confusion
It is an institution of illusion
God help them in Indianapolis
God help them in Minneapolis
But I will not shirk
I know how this does work
So I will not take flight
I will listen to the talks
I will visit the ballot box
Because, Uncle Sam I Am

An American

PUSH SLIDE TAP

Push, slide, tap
Where would I be without pointer finger
I could not look up google map
Over Facebook drama I could not linger

Push, slide, tap
I would miss my favorite shows
Photos I would not snap
Nothing to do but count my toes

Push, slide, tap
What about my games
I'm such a sentimental sap
The pigs must go up in flames

Push, slide, tap
It's free app Friday
I can download free crap
Help me off the internet highway

Push, slide, tap
This is more than just a fad
Freedoms wings I cannot flap
Good Lord, I'm addicted to my I-pad

FACEBOOK

Facebook diatribe
I can no longer abide
Appreciate your passion
But where is your compassion
For a world filled with adversity
Can't you delight in diversity
Your view's monocular
Your attitude jocular
Right-wing, left-wing
Long live the King
Realist, idealist
Fundamentalist, existential nihilist
Pick a side, choose
I refuse
Your words are meant to incite
It's either black or white
But I only see in shades of grey
Ignorance is all that you convey
So without further delay
From my page I wipe away
No trace, not a vestige
Of your negative message
So enjoy your reign
On some other plane
Go on a rampage
On some other stage
As for me and mine
We live sublime

FLESHY SHELL

Underneath this fleshy shell
So many stories to tell

Beauty on the outside can deny
Decay on the inside that would horrify

A body covered with scars
Could be hiding superstars

If you look with more than your eyes
Your opinions you might revise

Hear their words, laughter, cries
Even their silence may help you realize
That you should never stigmatize

Walk in another's shoes
If they don't have feet
Don't retreat
Get a clue
Crawl

SELF CHATTER

Can't take the abuse

The constant criticism

Need to call a truce

On the never-ending cynicism

You throw the words with easy scorn

You killer of dreams

Their death I can only mourn

And with their demise, follows my self-esteem

You have some nerve

Degrading, debasing, demeaning

Saying I don't deserve…

Embracing

Your perceptions are askew

Not based on fact

Simply not true

Evidence not backed

Give me a break

I can't get any clearer

You need a double take

You are not who I view in the mirror

Let's get to the crux of the matter

You…I…must stop

The negative self-chatter

IT FOLLOWED ME HOME

Mom, please it followed me home
Look at its sweet little face
I'll take care of it I swear

Its coat I will comb
I will make it a place
We have room to spare

Yes, I remember the snake
But it's cuddlier than that
Better than bugs

We cannot forsake
This little cat
For it... I'll give hugs

I will wash behind my ears
I will clean my room without complaint
Yes, I will hold still in church

Let me relieve your fears
I will be a saint
This ends my search

I've found the perfect playmate

You say it can stay

It's time to celebrate

What's that about renovate

Wait, what price to pay

We must relocate

I think I can be happy living in the shed

HOUSE CATS

House Cats
Noble creatures
Not exactly King of the jungle
But we shall say miniature Monarchs
Their athletic abilities
Give way to sayings such as
Catlike reflexes
Cat-walk
Their cries
Cat-call
Caterwaul
Inventions named after them
Catapult
Cat-scan
Their tendency for mischief
Gave way to words like
Catastrophe
Cataclysm
Their penchant for sloth
Catnap
One might surmise
A deity status
With their nine lives
Hard to say who owns whom
When we Cater
To their whims
Anyway you Categorize it
They rule!

EFFORT

I don't understand,
Why I have not won the lottery.
What's this nonsense about having to buy a ticket?

I don't understand,
Why I have not won a Pulitzer.
You say I have to be published first?

I don't understand,
Why success eludes my grasp.
Maybe I was afraid to reach?

I don't understand,
What it takes to have your dreams come true.
I guess I do, it's called.. effort!

WAR OF THE STREETS

"What's the prognosis?"

"The damage is extensive, expensive
it's true, but she'll pull through."

"At the risk of being obtuse,
you need to stop the abuse!"

"Don't you think I know?
This has taken its toll,
on her body.... and my soul."

"I have no choice, I have a job,
I have obligations, destinations,
I have a life!"

"But this is the second time,
I don't think she can survive a third,
and frankly, you don't have the dime."

"We have no choice....."

On to the weathered roads we go,
Praying not to pay the toll.
Serpentine down the scarred streets,

Not wanting to admit defeat.
Trying fiercely to avoid the cannibalistic holes.

Evidence of other's lost battles, litter the curbs.
No one escapes, city proper, nor suburbs.

Who's to blame?
For the pitted paths,
Winter's wrath?
King and Country?

It matters not
The conflict was fought,
and today...I made it home.

OLD WAYS

Even when it's good for you
There is grief in habits loss
For old ways I weep
It's not as easy as trash we toss

Toss in the garbage can
Like yesterday's newspaper
For old ways I weep
They stick like flypaper

Flypaper trapping, sticking
Keeping us mired down
For old ways I weep
In tears I may drown

Drown in self pity
But now in success, resuscitate
For new ways I keep
Now the controller of my fate

LESS THAN

The struggle
To be accepted
For who we are
Warts and all
Not who people
Want us to be
The perfect mother
The perfect teacher
The perfect wife
The perfect friend
Always I fall short
It gets harder
Each time
I leap again
Hoping
For a different outcome
Hoping for success
Or recognized
For the valiant effort
The quest continues
For the elusive
Perfect
But less than
For now
Is all I got

RESPECT: TO HOLD IN HIGH REGARD

"You will respect me!"
They shout with pistol in hand outstretched.
Pain in their face is etched.
But what they receive is not what they sought.
Fear is what they got.
It is an animal of a different color.
Its' stripes much duller.
Respect is to hold in high regard.
Starring down a barrel makes that hard.
A gun doesn't make one see you with esteem.
Admiration it does not bring.
Respect cannot be forced.
It cannot be coerced.
It is a concept to discern.
Put into action and earned.
Violence is only a false pose,
Like a cocky bird's crows.
No homage does it pay?
No demons does it slay.
It does not erase pain,
Only causes more disdain.
Put the guns away.
The answer in us lay.
In order to be free,
You need to shout, "I must respect me!"

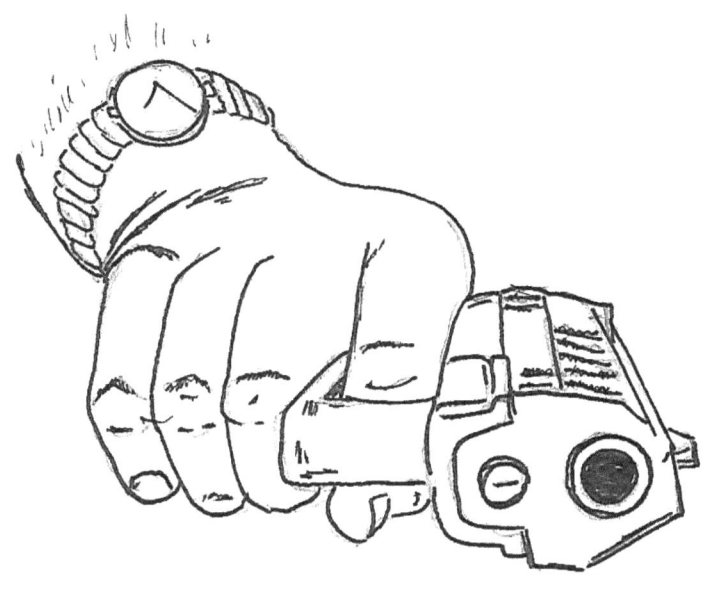

POTENTIAL

I use to be cocky.
Thought I would
Never be so weak as
To contemplate leaving
This corporeal realm.
But, as the years went by,
I have entertained such
Ideations.
Life circumstances has a way
Of wearing you down, like
Water does rock.
That said,
Life…life…LIFE
Has potential, opportunities,
Death….
Does not….
Cannot….
Provide or elicit change.

PERSEVERE

Life is a struggle
Your efforts must double
To keep you head above water

The world wants to slaughter
Turn your dreams into fodder
Like a welder you must solder
And strengthen your resolve

It's easy to solve
You must evolve
Negativity dissolve
Your mistakes absolve
Courage in the face of adversity

Lessons from the hard-knock University
Live a life of diversity
And persevere, yeah persevere

DON'T TALK CRAP

Mick
Spick
Nigger
Words that trigger
Idiot
Dork
Retard
Ignoring them is hard
Skank
Ho
Tart
Language that breaks your heart
Tears down your spirit
Sets you apart
From others it ostracizes
Who you are it criticizes
Queer
Fag
Names that tag
You as undesirable
Something less
Than the rest
Mackerel smacker
Rag head
Tree hugger

Hate is alive

It is a deep well

In which we all dwell

Way to much

Both as the deliverer

And the receiver

Slurs damage

It is a double edge sword

That cuts both

Avoid the self-destructive trap

Don't talk crap!

I MOVE LIKE A TURTLE

I move like the Turtle
Slow and steady
But my mind is fertile
Sown with imagination
Fearful of stagnation
I cling to my dreams
With willful determination

The rat race
Backing the hare
Insisting on the pace
Running past the crawling
Fear of stalling
Makes them miss out
No memories for recalling

I move like the Turtle
My heart devoted
To getting over the hurdle
Still in the marathon
Conclusion not forgone
I will endure
I will walk-on

THE TROUBLE WITH CAN'T

Their wings are not made aerodynamically
Scientist said about the bumblebee
They fly anyway.

That's not real art
They said to Picasso
His work is revered by millions.

That's not a real word
They said to Edger Allen Poe
"It is now," he replied.

That's not a weapon
One skeptic said to the martial artist
He recanted after he woke up.

The trouble with can't
Is that you need only
Remove the T and you can!

CAROUSEL

Time to get off the carousel
It's been a fun ride
Time to go out with the tide
To all a farewell

I started the walk in solitude
This is what I learned
This is what was discerned
That my view was skewed

For we are not alone
No matter how we try to hide
I must confide
That doubt is our millstone

Let your voice be heard
Let your light shine
Grasp your hand with mine
Cause something in my soul has stirred

And the journey is better shared

I GET UP

I get up
And paste on a counterfeit smile
Like one would apply makeup
I answer the polite question
"How are you doing?"
With false joviality
"Great"
I say with pretense
Inside my screams echo
Slamming against the locked
Room I so carefully guard
Somewhere I've garnered
Don't show weakness
They will rip you apart
Not quite sure who they are
But I am observant
I see stigma attached to others
Others that let the pain be seen
I was a soldier once
I understand the concept
Pull yourself up by your bootstraps
My straps are frayed and worn
I imagine they will snap soon
Leaving me to traverse
Barefoot across the hot coals

Pain is my constant companion

And is a taxing familiarity

One I wish to divest myself of

But it is like a tumor

Wrapped around a vital organ

"Try this pill, "says the Dr.

"Will it take the pain away?"

"No, but it will take away the depression."

I lift my brow

"So.. You're saying I will be happily in pain?"

Serious doubts

Night is coming

Restless sleep at best

And then

I get up

WHEN

When does it get easier
When do I know my own heart
Why are there days of crystal clarity
Why are they such a rarity

All I seek is truth
To see with more than just my eyes
Why is that so controversial
Shouldn't it be universal

Each person seeing their own reality
Life according to _____
The facts elusive
Not at all conclusive

When is wisdom a given
When does it not sift through brain cells like sand
Why are we not equipped
With life's manuscript

Too much to contemplate
The answers will have to wait
Problem's minefield I will have to navigate
Like a GPS I will recalculate
And keep on seeking the right path.

CONTROL

We all seek control
Of notions, emotions
It is a common goal

We all seek control
Over our aspirations, situations
It's just how we roll

We all seek control
Even of others
In our schemes we enroll

We all seek control
Sometimes to be disappointed
When we fall into a sinkhole

We all seek control
Only to elude our grasp
Hang on to your soul

We all seek control
But the only thing you can bankroll
Is the seeking itself

POETRY

Poetry

Like water

Takes more than one form

Words on a page, black ink on white paper

A stark contrast.

The spoken art that trickles off a speaker's tongue

Like water across the rocks in a stream

Or on the haunting lyrics of a

Troubadour's melody

Water in its liquid state

Falling from the sky

Nourishing the Earth

Just as soliloquy can quench

A parched soul

The harden form of ice

Used to reduce an angry wound

Just as the correct prose

Can soothe an inflamed temper

Steam utilized in ceremony

To excise one's demons

Just as a dirge might be dispensed

To clear the doldrums

So.....

Yes, poetry

Like water

Is powerful

And necessary

WRITER'S BLOCK

Dear writer's block
It's not you, it's me
No, I do not Mock
I hear your plea
But have found another
One who fuels creativity
One who will not smother
It's time to shed negativity

You are comfortable it's true
But you need to move on
I'm tossing you like an old shoe
I will not listen to the con
Imagination has broken free
A new hat I've don
In life no longer an absentee

Dear writer's block
You are now a divorcee
In my path no longer a rock
You owe me an apology
For trying to trip me up
I've found my zen
I will not drink from your cup
In my hand the return of the pen

TO WRITE OR NOT TO WRITE?

To write or not to write? That is the question:

Whether it is feeble in the mind to suffer

The red ink and marks of outrageous correction,

Or take pen in hand against a sea of critics.

And by opposing condemn them? To read, to think

No more; and by <u>think</u> to say we end

The heartache and the thousand bad novels

That the public is heir to, 'tis an epilogue

Devoutly to be wished,

To create, to write:

To write, perchance to publish - ay, there's the rub:

For in those words what dreams may come,

When we have submitted to one hundred publishers?"

THE TREE

Right off school property

The canopy ringed with a cigarette haze
Maybe something else that left you in a daze

I had to walk fast
To get past

To return home unscathed
Despite the insults in which I was bathed

A no-mans land
A place to make a stand

Raise a fisted hand
Or fall face first in the sand

Invitation to join those that ruled
Into the kingdom of cool

But alas I marched to a different beat
One that would not retreat

Neither a leader nor follower be
My spirit needed to be free

Those others under the delusion
That inclusion
Brought about coveted gifts
like independence or control

Those I already possessed
By not being like the rest
My only request

Was respect

Which was finally obtained
When they tried to detain
And a good punch was aimed

They admitted I was nobody's fool
And a right hook was a good tool

I learned
That not all lessons are acquired in school

THE TRUTH OF THE MATTER

I laid-my money on the fortuneteller's table.
He said, "You and your money will soon part."

Still another day, I tried again.
"You will struggle with obesity."
I questioned, "The cards told you that? "
"No," the ornately-clad soothsayer replied.
"I smelled the hamburger and onions on your breath. "

I'm a slow learner.

Yet another day found me at the door of a gypsy wagon.
The thick massacred woman told me,
"The tea leaves say you will find Love tonight. "
Indeed I did, if not my own,
as I watched the entwined couple under the street lamp,
on my walk home.

Another try, my palm outstretched.
"Will I live a long life? "
"Compared to a butterfly, yes.
 Compared to a redwood tree, no. "

I sat on a curb,
Head in my hands.
Feeling uncertain about my future.
I felt a hand on my shoulder.
A fellow earth traveler
Took a seat next to me.
I told him my woes.
He asked if he could share
The truth of the matter.
I nodded assent.

The truth of the matter is;
If you Love,
You will find love.
If you find love
You will be richer than most.
And time is irrelevant,
To those who've loved
And have been loved.
As for obesity,
Choose the salad

August 2009

Therese M. Guy

THE DEATH OF DREAMS

Some say it is the dawn that murders dreams,

That they are fragile things.

Like a castle built of sand.

And with natures hand,

An imagined prince the war concedes,

As the morning tide's wave recedes.

Others say it is mans words that are the slayer.

Those negative nay-sayers.

I say we imprison of our own free will,

Ideas we pass sentence to kill.

It is fear that waters the seed,

That grows and chokes like a weed.

That is the demise of the dream conceived.

Death could have been staved, if only we believed.

SLEEPLESS

Sleepless nights
Interrupted by
Shadowed frights

Pleasant dreams
Disturbed by
Haunting screams

Sheets hold tight
In their grip
Restless legs that fight

The clock's steady beat
Like a metronome
Keeps tracks of sand mans retreat

Life's daily stress
Squeezes
The heart in distress

Starry sky's
give way to
baggy eyes

Another test
Of my fortitude
To tackle all—with little rest

SLEEP

Sleep
My elusive lover,
Robs me of his sweet embrace.
Murders my dreams.
With the stealth of a ninja,
He poisons my system,
And my body twist and turns,
Tangling in my funeral shroud.
My cries to be rescued,
"Sandman"
Go unheeded.
Oh to feel his loving caress,
To revel in his touch,
Just drift away,
In silent ecstasy.
But he is a no show,
I think we are headed,
For divorce!

FAMILY PHOTOS

Youthful parental photos
Mirroring your own features
Connecting you to your roots
Your Father's hairline
Your Mother's smile
Moments frozen
Small glimpses to the past
Two-dimensional images
Drawing forth
Three-dimensional feelings
Yearning for one more touch
Or perhaps a missed word
"I'm sorry."
"I'm proud."
"I love you."
The flat paper image falls short
Yet the viewers' fingers
Slowly glide over it
Caressing it, and trying
To absorb a connection
Realization dawns
The picture is only a catalyst
The true connection
Is in your heart

IRELAND

She called to me
In my imaginings
In my Bones
In my Heart
She Called to Me
And I answered
She did not disappoint
The cliffs
The moors
The music
That speaks to my soul
She called to me
Drawing me home
Holding me tight
To her bosom
She called to me
In my sleep
In my dreams
Till I could not but answer
I missed you, she said
And when I reached
Her shores
I breathed her in
The familiar scent
Of a loving mother
She called to me
And I came home

Heavy Load

Heavy load
False accusations
Shoulders bowed
Riotous condemnation

Knees buckle
Heart wrenches
Bleeding knuckles
Determination entrenches

Individual millstone
Weighing down
Wearing to the bone
Thorny crown

Encrusted flayed skin
Mixed with contempt and spit
Endured to save men
All sin acquit

Paying the ultimate price
Laying down His life
Himself a sacrifice
So we may join in paradise

IN THE COURTYARD

The Truth resides
Within my breast
Would I too deny
Would I pass the test
Or would I Lie
"I'm not with Him"
Out loud I cry
And in saying so
It becomes truth

GRATITUDE

Some dread the holidays
They treat it like a malaise

Fearing inflated expectations
Worrying about money limitations
Strength sapping celebrations
Irritating family relations

I look forward them
Like receiving a precious gem

I'm like a petulant child
Anger raging wild

I'm in need of a time out
In the corner while I pout
Let me scream and shout
Time to think about

A grandchild's hug
A coffee-filled mug
A warm soak in the tub
A sore back rub

A wrong forgiven
That I'm still liven

That arm around me in my sorrow
The meal I'm sharing tomorrow

Yes I need a Time Out
To adjust my attitude
To remember gratitude

Join me
Blessed Be

MY MOTHER'S DISHES

My mother's dishes
Sitting on dusty cabinet shelves
Forgotten dreams and wishes

Rings and things
In oversized jewelry boxes
Secrets kept in sealed lockets

Chest of photos
Beauty fading, smiles frozen
In albums cracked and yellowed

Letters in shoeboxes
Wrapped in ribbon
Residing in the back of closets

Bronzed baby shoe
Pressed flowers in a book
Ancient newspaper residue

Memorabilia grasping at eternity
Holding hands with us in our fraternity
Joining us in our mortality

MY MOTHER'S CLOSET

Grief washes over me,
like a tidal wave on an eroding beach.
As I step into her closet,
I am awash with memories.
She wore that one on her 50th
wedding anniversary celebration.
She bought that one on our girls
day out to the mall trip.
There is the bathrobe I would
wrap her in as I helped her
in her bathing ritual the last
year of her life.
It smells like her, like lilac and
honeysuckle, the sensation is to
much and a physical pain emerges
in the center of my chest as I choke
and sputter with rivers of tears running
down my cheeks.
Oh, oh, I must not soil my mother's
clothes. "Get it together, I say in my mind."
Then I glance at her beautiful, tiny
size 4 shoes and I must step out
of the closet or surely be lost in
the enormity of the loss of
my mother, my mother, momma!

Sept. 2000 t.m.c..

ONCE I WAS BEAUTIFUL.

Once, I was beautiful

Once,
I had thick, unruly,
wavy hair.

Once,
I had curves
Not model thin
Never, model thin
But Marilyn Monroe
voluptuous

Once,
My eyes were bright
and my skin tone
taunt and color even

Once, I was beautiful
I almost missed it
Having never known
until now,
that once, I was beautiful.

Now,
my hair is
streaked with silver

Now,
I have mass with rolls
Not morbidly obese
Never, morbidly obese
But Mae West rotund

Now,
My eyes are wise
And my skin
weathered and creased

Now, I am beautiful
I almost missed it
Until now.

Shannon Crossbear ©2008

THE ULTIMATE BETRAYAL

The ultimate betrayal

If my stomach had lips

It would give me a Judas kiss

If my knees were in the service

They would be brought up on charges

For desertion

Likewise, my mind would be AWOL

My skin shirks its duty

My eyes have been practicing sabotage

My body

Once my closest friend

Has become a traitor

The ultimate betrayal

QUARANTINE

Under quarantine
6 feet in between
The Agony
The Calamity
Trying to bare the tragedy
Now I understand
Sun and moon pass by
But never touch
No sweet embrace
No saving grace
Love unrequited
The world blighted
Loneliness highlighted
Abdicating to a virus
Relinquishing a piece of the soul
To fear

Like a prisoner
With a visitor
Hands raised on
Opposite sides of glass
Seeking connection
Amid Isolation
A wave is nice
But does not suffice
Under quarantine
6 feet in between
In dire need
Of a vaccine

FLU

Size does not matter

microscopic organisms have laid me flat

Taken me down on the mat

Sinus infection a worthy adversary

When in the throes of its nasty grip

You swear at stake is your very mortality

Should I call the mortuary

More likely the apothecary

Chicken soup for the croup

Willow bark tea

To make the fever flee

Those things in my weapons armory

Doc says death is not the reality

But, I beg to differ

It is my sniffer

That robs me of the breath of life

Causing, oh so much strife

He reiterates REST

Who has time to do anything other than whine

Wine, I remember now

Alcohol stifles according to scientific research

Back to the mortuary

Heading for the cemetery

Preserved before embalming

Gonna drown those cold germs!

WORDS

My dog doesn't bite
My kid wouldn't fight
Famous last words
I never.....
I always.....
Sooner or later you
Will be eating those words
I hate.....
A word better left unsaid
I love you…..
An underused word
I can't…..
A defeating word
I can…..
A powerful word
Words start wars
Words reunite
Think before you speak

Negative Posts

Like a disease
These negative posts
Have entered my system
Causing coronary occlusion

Disillusion ensues
Spreading from the heart
To the brain
Confusion reigns

Maintains Mayhem
Networking savagely
Throughout your being
Poisoning views

Skews perceptions
Truth --- Fake
Makes my stomach ache
It seems to incite

Ignite my primal fears
Flight or fight
But who to fight
I need to disengage

Assuage my poor soul
Take deep breaths
Pick my battles
And post more cat video

TRAVELER

Never have I traveled further
Than on my present journey
Introspection
Circumspectrum
The path rocky
Preconceived notions
Block me
Demons stock me
Mock me
The demons have names;
Regret
Sorrow
Disappointment
But there are aid stations
Along the way too
With helpers called
Resilience
Fortitude
Appreciation
I have a few blisters
Weathered a few twisters
Fell down onto despair
Invoked God in prayer
Rose up
And set about repair
Still traveling
Maybe a few flooded roads
Still ahead
But...
I brought galoshes

MIDWEST

As a youth, I bemoaned my Midwest roots
Crying at endless boring plains
Life took me on many pursuits
Far enough I could break the chains

Chains that held me fast
I thought they stifled
The change of heart I could not forecast
The preconceived notions rifled

Rifled through my heart
Distance does make it grow fonder
The longer we were apart
Faded the desire to wander

Wander from the tall green corn
The friendly neighbor waves
The sunrise in the early morn
I must give the soul what it craves

Craves the home it came from
As I matured
I no-longer saw humdrum
The wanderlust was cured

Cured of discontent
I have returned
Time away I do not lament
Midwest, never again spurned

APRIL'S FOOLS

The alarm goes off at 3 am
That is the start
To the day where joking is a fine art
I lay back down and just end up tossin'
I know I must approach the day with caution
I check the shampoo
Last year it turned my hair blue
Yep, the toilet is clear
No cellophane barrier to fear
My hubby offers me breakfast
Suspicion rules,
"No, thanks, I can handle the task."
I turn the phone ringer off
What---you scoff
Last year they called
And said I won ten grand
I had such plans
I heavily suggest skepticism
As a defense mechanism
I don't know how you feel
But I don't think I can deal
Courage I lack
I know where to head
My covers I pull back
Good Lord—who short-sheeted my bed!

CROSSWORDS

Twenty four across
A salty Chinese condiment
"Soy Sauce"

Thirty four down
A Town within a city
"China Town"

Crosswords
A hunt of a different kind
Work that brain, that big muscle

How many ways to say the same thing
Hang, adhere, stick, cling
A fountain of knowledge, a well spring

And I only checked the back of the book
A couple of times
Fraud, cheat, scam, poser

OUT HOUSE

Through the tall pines, snowflakes crisply sounding underfoot, icy crunch.
Evenings breeze on the branches softly whispers.
Moonlight's path shadowed in snow clouds full billowed like ship sails forming.
As if on queue Big Lake waves their bass tempo churning with each crash ashore.

Creak goes the old hinges, those old bones too.
What a wondrous and pondering travel in the woods beheld, short its wonder, it's true.
To a place of simple relief to any who venture or respite this way, night or day, throughout the years.

Like a weather-shielded port from the storm, this ole lighthouse of refuse, humble yet strong-hearted it stands. Having withstood the tides of time, nature, and her Furry furies too, still proudly stands a testament to the needs of man overcome by engineering skills.

In this place of great view, scribbling on walls forbidden…
If you're reading this scribbling the you too …
Have made the journey to our simple Loo…In the big woods on the North Lake Superior.

Remember to lock the door when leaving… thank you.

New Year

The New Year is
Like taking a shower after a hard days toil
Washing off the previous year's dirt
Weariness' death grip foiled
Scrubbing away my hearts turmoil
Trying not to revert
The last vestiges rinsed down the drain
Vigor replaces lethargy
Nourishing the soul like a spring rain
A new outlook, a new campaign
Reinvent, refresh, renew, with energy

EMPTY WELL

I thought the well ran dry
But, that was fear's lie

No excuses, no alibi
Watch me defy

Hear my war cry
I hereby notify

I have plenty more to say
Quite the array

Plain or fancy wordplay
Thirst I will allay

Dispelling dismay
I'm here to stay

THE FENCE WALKER

I'm a fence walker.
I want to sit on the fence,
But traffic makes that impossible.
I use to have rose-colored glasses,
That helped some.
Those are long gone,
And vertigo assaults me.
Balance is precarious,
Realist, Idealist,
Left-wing, Right-wing,
Fundamentalist, Existential Nihilist,
Pick a side.
I refuse!
I continue my tight rope act.
No equilibrium problems for some,
It's either Black or White,
But, I only see in shades of Grey.
Sweet and Sour,
Fact or Fiction,
Ying and Yang,
Give and Take,
The path is slippery,
And I wobble a lot.
I struggle for equipoise,
A Happy Medium,

Therein lies the rub,

Happy is the other end to sad.

There is just medium,

No Happy to be attached.

One thing is clear,

It is a lonely path.

Whitewashed battlement

Stands firm against the tirade

Of mans arrogance

I RUN WITH A GANG

I run with a gang
Pain jumped me in
Frustration reigns

Surviving initiation
Was only the beginning
Age brought about escalation

From this pack
I wish to disassociate
But they say no going back

Follow into the depths of despair
Sleepless nights wracked with pain
This situation just not fair

Empty promises of, "you're not alone."
Please give me hope
Throw the dog a bone

From this malady set me free
Break the chains of this suffering
God above hear my plea

No more the need to endure
Take my hand in yours
Bring about the cure

From my sins I do atone
If you deem
Remove this millstone

I USED TO BE STRONG

I used to think
I was strong
Because I have endured
Great physical trials
I use to think
I was strong
Because others relied on me
I use to think
I was strong
Because I was a soldier once
I use to think
I was strong
Because I was a martial artist
I use to think
I was strong
Because I had faith
When it was no longer fashionable
I use to think.........
But mere words
Have brought me to my knees
Showed me the truth
I am weakness personified
Your tongue is sharper
Than a sword
And has wounded my soul
Drained my strength
I ceded my power
Fortitude depleted
I use to think
I was strong
But emotional abuse

Reigned supreme

WINTER'S TOUCH

Winter's hand has come calling.
From the eaves--icicle fingers reach.
Their cold touch--like death
Into its grasp, I'm falling.

What happened to Earth's warm embrace?
Was it all a calumny?
Mother Nature's vile trick.
Does she mock me to my face?

As the bitter wind does blow,
I endeavor to resist.
To the snow Queen, I will not bow,
Even as the trees bend low.

How will frost's sharp bite I stave?
Indoor sports I will play.
With my lover--beneath the sheets,
I will find the heat I crave.

ORDINARY LIFE

I have lived a life

Nothing grand

No Oscars

No fame

But, I've had extra-ordinary moments

I've tasted an orange

I've seen a sunset

No athletic records

No heroic medals

But, I've had magic moments

A first kiss

A child within

No decedent riches

No fancy titles

But, I've had incredible experiences

A flute played alone in a forest

A black belt worn proudly

Perhaps no giant impact

Yes, an ordinary life

But, filled with extra-ordinary beauty

TEA PARTY

He sat crossed legged
On the ground
The delicate porcelain cup
At odds
In his large calloused hands
Did he know
Did he foresee
It was more than just tea
A daughter's cherished memory
No…More profound
A legacy
"Yes, please."
His rough voice boomed a bit too loud
As he accepted her offer
Of an imaginary drop of honey
His participation worth
More than money
The gift
An ideal of how a man should be
Yes, it was more than just tea

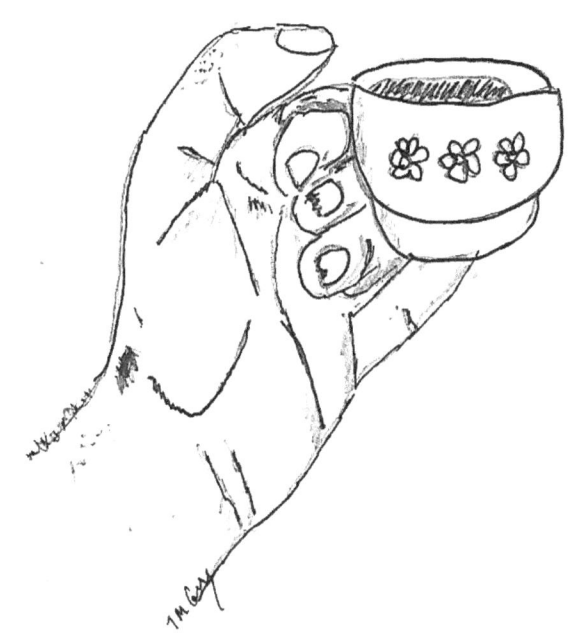

CHALK

Chalk, bubbles
Forgetting my troubles
Little sandpiles
Inside the door
from emptied shoes

Songs, stories
Of past glories
Passed along
To willing
Little ears

Kites, tire swings
How to make fairy wings
Kisses and hugs
Their hands in mine
Warming my heart

Completely beguiled
Special each child
Energy renewed
From every endearment
Grandma, I love you

CRAYON MARKS

Crayon marks on the wall
Toys scattered down the hall
little people in the home
I must confess
can be a stress

"Grandma, tie my shoe."
"Can I come too?"
"She hit me first."
"I'm done!"
"Come wipe my bum"

But not to despair
They're pluses to spare
To having them around
A hug, a kiss, a hand in mine
Is like the sunshine

So when I need a rest
From all the mess
I will recall
Their words so true
"Grandma I Love You"

SUPER HEROES

Everyday Super Heroes

No caped crusader here
Just a cape that needs mending

No masked vigilante
Just a face etched with wrinkles

No death-defying deeds
Just a daily determination to get the job done

No genetic enhancements
Just a few scars

No mind-reading abilities
Just a heart filled with empathy

No truth determining Lasso
Just a great sense of integrity

No high flying spider webs
Just a safety harness that keeps one from falling

No larger than life muscles
Just grit and strong will

No speed like a bullet
Just a slow, steady gait

No power shield
Just laughter that deflects pain

Teen Turtles, Green Arrows or Muscles,
Fast as a Flash, or a speeding bullet
These are not real

Custodians, Firefighters, Teachers
Stay at home moms,
Doctors
These are the real deal

Lycra tights not required
Just a willingness of their gifts to share
Of lending a hand, or give a care

Just look around
Everyday heroes abound

After the Parades

After the parades
After the ticker tape falls
When the public no longer recalls
Sacrifices made
What then?
What then?
After the yellow ribbons come down
After the welcome home kisses
When you're filled in on the misses
Too many to count
What then?
 What then?
After the bumper stickers cannot be read
After the handshakes fade
When Normal is a façade
Just a charade
What then?
What then?
After the handshakes stop
And the scars still remain
And you're in so much pain
To hard to bear
What now?
What now?

EVERY GENERATION

It happens every generation
The winter dare
The irresistible inclination
Gullible beware
Resist the temptation

Don't let tongue and metal meet
You must resist
Fate you cannot cheat
There are better things kissed
From this dare retreat

But Alas, there is always one
Who must always test
Yep, I should have run
I should have acquiesced
I would not be outdone

Let idiocy reign
How do you bandage a tongue
Oh---the pain
My bravery unsung
False dignity I still maintain

For the winter dare
I swear
Is a right of passage

All of Those

The forest creatures found the object by the brook.
"What is it?" asked rabbit.
"Power," the red fox answered in a reverent tone.
"Knowledge," said the wise old owl.
"Adventure," squealed the squirrel.
"Entertainment," the otter added.
'Mystery," ventured the crow.
"Love," cooed the turtledoves.
"All of those sillies," giggled the little girl,
as she picked up her book, sat down, and began to read.

IT'S A GOOD LIFE

Yes, it's a good life, and it's the small things that make it so.
The big things hurt my head.
My atheist friends think I'm stupid for believing in things unseen.
My religious friends think I'm going to Hell in a handbasket.
My conservative friends think I don't deserve health care.
My Liberal friends think I should give away what little I have.
My patriotic friends think I should shake every soldier's hand.
(I served; every soldier is not exactly hero material.)
My indigenous friends think I should fly the flag upside down.
In a favorite movie of mine, the cowboy character endures untold hardships,
and tragedies. As he is lying on the prairie looking up at a star-filled evening sky,
He says, "It is a good life, when it ain't raining or snowing."
I agree, it's a good life:
When I get a hug from a friend for no reason.
When I play my flute in an echo filled canyon.
When I watch the firefly's' dance in my backyard tree.
When someone I hurt forgives me.
When I bite into a strawberry.
When I get a shower after a sweaty workout.
Yes, it's a good life,
When I get in my car and see the little dancing flower on my dash.

I MARRIED A PIRATE

He's got that swagger
In his hand a dagger
Cutlass by his side
By the stars he did navigate
Destined by fate
To sail into my heart
There were rough patches
But we'd batten down the hatches
And weather the storm
Lay anchor in calm waters
Take solace in our daughters
And continue the adventure
I'll tend the wheel
With great zeal
Cause I married a Pirate Man

FRIENDS ARE LIKE SHOES

Friends are like Shoes
Some are like...
That favorite pair of tennis shoes
They paid their dues
Forever in your heart
Some are like...
Your best dress shoes
Not worn often, but
Always there for your special
Occasions
Some are like...
Pool shoes
Making sure you don't
Slip and drown
Some are like...
Sandals
Easy going and let's
You breathe.
I think I like...
Collecting shoes

BUCKET LIST

I could not resist
I made the list
You know the one in anticipation
Of when you kick the bucket
I felt that drive
To skydive
To swim with Dolphins
To learn a new language
I felt that compulsion
A need for propulsion
To reach for the stars
Ride in fast cars
Fly a kite
Go white water rafting
Not all is an adrenaline rush
I want to play my flute
In ancient cave dwellings
Write stories ripe for the telling
Sit by a fire, listening to katydids
Visit my ancestral home
To just get on my bike and roam
No impossible fantasies
Such as sing on American Idol
Or win a boxing title
Just live life to the fullest
Up to the very last minute
Check a few things off my list
Only in death I desist
Oh, and bury me with my bucket

CHOOSE

Choose
My girls were in a fight
They each said they could not live with the other
They asked me to choose
Claiming I loved or babied the other more
Choose
You have got to be kidding
That's like asking
Choose
whether you want to die
From lethal injection
Or the gas chamber
Neither,
I would not want to die
Choose
between those I brought into this world
is asking me to die
Choose
I did to bring you both into this world
To love you even when your words or deeds
Tore holes in my heart
Even when you pointed out my flaws as a parent
Which I'm sure are many
But I cannot concede that
Not choosing is a flaw

Choose

I'm sorry, but I do not love you

The same

I love the eldest beautiful voice,

Her ability to focus, her ability to obtain goals.

I love the youngest fondest of God's creatures,

Her spontaneity, her imagination

Choose

I love you equally but different

There is no choice

You can choose

Choose

To accept each other's flaws, or

Choose

To walk away

Choose

To try one more time

Choose

The harder but higher path

Because, you see, mine

Was an iron-clad contract

That cannot be rescinded

Even in the midst of discord

I choose you both.

BOB AND WEAVE

Duck, bob, weave
Evade, move, block
Muscles tighten like rock
So I do not receive
That well-placed kick
That fated blow
Opponent promises to bestow
Wish I was controlled by a joystick
My administrator skilled
Making me jump, fly, flip
But alas, it is not so
I should have swerved
Instead of dip, if I had
I might have preserved
My dignity and pride
Instead it resides
On the floor, along
With my backside

Heading to the Y

So you had a bad day

A bad week

Don't admit defeat

Get up off the street

Start again

It's better than

Where you've been

Pushing up

Is good exercise

Your strength will surprise

Mistakes are a part

Of the process

On the road to success

You can obtain

Your dreams come to fruition

Hard work is the tuition

With that

I'm heading to the Y

FIRE SPINNING

It wasn't a lark
That little spark
In my imagination
I fanned the flame
No longer tame
It saved me from stagnation
It became a blaze
Inhibitions it razed
I did not cower
Off came restraints
No longer feint
Before fire's power
Oh, what a high
To let fear die
And to control
Something powerful as Sol

TEACHER

The teacher looked out at the class
One head is down on his desk
One hand in the air asking," Will there be a test."
One more asks for a hall pass

The instructor says a silent prayer
Help me reach their minds
Golden nuggets of knowledge finds
Their hearts and souls to care

What does it take to instill
Love of learning
Knowledge yearning
This tasks takes skill

Is it a war of attrition
Wear them down like water on rocks
Or learn by the school of hard knocks
To win the battle, what ammunition

The bell rings
One student lingers
Shyly playing with her fingers
She reveals, "when I read, my heart sings."

The educator no longer in despair
If just for one, the light is on
Then hopelessness is not forgone
No other job can compare

THERESE GUY is a Midwesterner who grew up in a family who loved the written word. She equates her writing style similar to humorist Erma Bombeck. She has short stories and poems published in the *Chicken Soup for the Soul* series. Therese owned and operated a Martial Arts studio for forty years. She is an Army Veteran and mother of two. She resides in Omaha, Nebraska, with her husband and several furred friends. You can find more about her or other books in the works on her blog, Thereseguy.blogspot.com.

www.ingramcontent.com/pod-product-compliance
Lightning Source LLC
Chambersburg PA
CBHW031943070426
42450CB00006BA/781